O9-ABI-800

Snap
books®

Friendship
Quizzes

How Much Do You Know about Bullying?

by Jen Jones

Consultant:
Stephanie Goerger Sandahl, MA, LPC
Clinical Specialist
Generations, Inc. Counseling Associates

CAPSTONE PRESS
a capstone imprint

Snap Books are published by Capstone Press,
151 Good Counsel Drive, P.O. Box 669, Mankato, Minnesota 56002.
www.capstonepub.com

Books published by Capstone Press are manufactured with paper
containing at least 10 percent post-consumer waste.

Library of Congress Cataloging-in-Publication Data
Jones, Jen.
 How much do you know about bullying? / by Jen Jones ; consultant,
Stephanie Goerger Sandahl.
    p. cm.—(Friendship quizzes)
 Includes index.
 Summary: A quiz about bullying
 ISBN 978-1-4296-6540-7 (library binding)
 1. Bullying—Juvenile literature. 2. Bullying in schools—Juvenile literature.
I. Title.
 BF637.B85J67 2012
 302.3—dc22   2011001570

Editor: Brenda Haugen
Designer: Veronica Correia
Media Researcher: Marcie Spence
Production Specialist: Laura Manthe

Alamy Images: AF Archive, 20 (top), Allstar Picture Library, 28 (top), Moviestore Collection
Ltd., 24 (top); Capstone Studio: Karon Dubke, cover, 6, 7 (bottom right), 8 (bottom), 10, 12,
15, 20 (bottom), 26, 28 (bottom); Shutterstock: Alice, (design element), Amy Myers, 19,
Apollofoto, 8 (top), ARENA Creative, 23, Ayelet Keshet, (design element), azzzya, (design
element), Blend Images, 16 (bottom), blue67design, (design element), Catalin Petolea, 18,
claudia veja, 14, Couperfield, 11 (bottom), Dana E. Fry, 9 (background), East, 16 (top), Elena
Elisseeva, 1, Elise Gravel, (design element), Kiselev Andrey Valerevich, 11 (top), koh sze
kiat, 9 (left), Kruchankova Maaike Boot, (design element), Maya, 4, mashe, 9 (right), mtr,
7 (bottom left), Olena Mykhaylova, 13, OLJ Studio, 24 (bottom), Primusoid, (design
element), Suzanne Tucker, 7 (top), Todd Castor, 22, Tom&Kwikki, (design element),
Tony Magdaraog, 7 (bottom middle), UltraViolet, (design element), zsooofija,
(design element)

Printed in the United States of America in Melrose Park, Illinois.
032011   006112LKF11

Table of Contents

Introduction

Bullying is a bigger issue than ever before. From TV to magazines to newspapers, it seems like stories about bullying are everywhere. You just can't seem to get away from it. Sometimes bullies hide behind their computers and terrorize others through cyberspace. At other times, they strike out with physical violence. Many young people deal with it all the time. In fact, six out of every 10 American teens see someone get bullied at least once a day. And that doesn't count the 3.7 million who are doing the bullying!

Ever wonder where you fit into this picture? This book will help you figure out whether you're a bully, a possible victim, a bystander, or a forever friend. The answer just might surprise you.

Even though this is nothing like taking a test at school (it's way cooler!), there are a few things you'll need before you get started. And don't worry—no #2 pencils required.

• Grab a sheet of notebook paper to write your answers down. You'll also need a pen or pencil. Number the sheet from 1 to 14, and you're ready to rock!

AND PLEASE, DO NOT WRITE IN THIS BOOK!!!

• Tell the truth. No one will see your answers but you.

OK ... ready, set, grow!

1- A new girl approaches your lunch table in hopes of sitting down. You:

a) Explain that this has been your group's special table forever, hoping she'll get the hint.

b) Let her sit down, but roll your eyes silently at your BFF across the table.

c) Say, "Sure, the more the merrier!" and ignore the angry looks from your friends.

2- You're dying to know who your pal is crushing on, but only your other friend knows the secret. What do you do?

a) Say nothing. Your pal will reveal her crush when she's ready.

b) Tell your friend that you'll broadcast her crush unless she dishes the dirt.

c) Share a juicy secret of your own in hopes that she'll feel obligated to fess up.

3- You ask a friend to go shopping after school. She says no, but you see her at the mall with another group of girls. What's your reaction?

a) You confront her in front of the other girls.

b) You quickly duck into a store and hope she doesn't see you.

c) You try not to cry when she sees you and ignores you.

4- When a rumor goes around, you tend to:

a) Believe it.

b) Hope that it's not about you.

c) Spread it.

5- It's time for swim team tryouts! You notice some of your teammates covering their mouths and laughing. You quickly realize they're laughing about how one girl looks in her swimsuit. You:

a) Crack a joke about how skinny that chick is. She looks like a twig!

b) Grab the nearest towel so they don't get a good look at you.

c) Can't help but laugh. It's contagious!

6- Birthday sleepover time! Your parents want you to invite all the girls in your class. How do you handle it?

a) You pass out the invites to everyone. However, you make it clear to those outside your circle they're only invited because your parents made you do it.

b) You cringe and wonder if you should tell your mom about the girl in class who has been picking on you.

c) You happen to "lose" a few of the invites. It's not your fault they got lost in the mail, right?

7- What bugs you the most about your friends?

a) When they act weird toward me, and I don't know why.

b) When they get all **clique**-y and leave me out.

c) When they don't do what I want.

8- You see someone being bullied outside of school. You:

a) Wonder what the victim did to deserve it.

b) Keep to yourself. After all, the bully could turn on you if you try to help.

c) Be thankful that it's not you this time.

11

9- Social media, IMs, texting, all that jazz—to you technology:

a) Is a fun way to get into mischief now and then.

b) Is scary. You never know what someone will post about you.

c) Lets me keep tabs on what everyone is doing.

10- How do you feel when you and your friends are in a fight?

a) It hurts my feelings, but I usually give in and say they were right.

b) Bring it! I'm not afraid of conflict.

c) I try to stay calm and figure out the best way to resolve things.

11- In the yearbook, you're most likely to be voted:

a) Queen Bee.

b) Best Personality.

c) Most likely to hide in her locker.

12- You and a few others are in competition for the lead role in the school play. One girl pressures you to drop out of the competition. You:

a) Drop out. It's not worth the hassle, and there will be other plays.

b) Casually mention to the competition that everyone thinks they would be better as understudies.

c) Figure all's fair in love and drama club! Whatever it takes to land the role, that's what you'll do.

13- When you get mad, you're most likely to:

a) Use the old silent treatment.

b) Get physical or call people names.

c) Keep it all inside. Getting mad will only get you in trouble.

14- As little kids, you used to hang out with your neighbor all the time. Now she's ignoring you. What do you do?

a) Continue to be nice and say, "Hi." Maybe she'll come around and be friends again.

b) People grow out of friendships all the time. I'll be able to deal.

c) Do whatever she does. Then maybe she'll be my friend again.

Don't turn the page yet!

It's time to tally your results. Check your answers below. Jot down the number of points you scored for each answer, and then add up your points.

1. a—1; b—2; c—3

2. a—3; b—1; c—2

3. a—1; b—2; c—3

4. a—2; b—3; c—1

5. a—1; b—3; c—2

6. a—1; b—3; c—2

7. a—2; b—3; c—1

8. a—1; b—2; c—3

9. a—1; b—3; c—2

10. a—2; b—1; c—3

11. a—1; b—2; c—3

12. a—3; b—2; c—1

13. a—2; b—1; c—3

14. a—3; b—1; c—2

Turn to page 18 if you scored 14 to 23 points.

Turn to page 22 if you scored 24 to 33 points.

Turn to page 26 if you scored 34 to 42 points.

RESULTS

BULLY ALLERT!

You love being the queen bee, but your sting may be more powerful than you realize.

The Full Scoop

Chances are you've probably teased, **excluded**, or hurt someone. You may have thought your behavior was all in good fun. Or maybe you didn't. Bullies often enjoy the feeling of power they get from being mean to others. But even if you thought your actions were all in fun, they weren't. You could be a bona fide bully. Bullying comes in many different forms, including physical, verbal, and cyber bullying. You might be a bully without realizing it. What you say, what you text, or what you post online can sometimes hurt as much as a punch. So does this make you a villain? No, of course not! It's never too late to make a change and say good-bye to the mean girl mentality.

Real-Life Rx: Tips You Can Use

• Why not use your power for good? After all, you're a leader. Others want to hear what you have to say. So set a positive tone. It's contagious!

• Remember the last time someone made you feel sad, lonely, or depressed. You'll be less tempted to bully someone again if you can put yourself in someone else's shoes.

• An apology goes a long way in making things right. Say "I'm sorry" to someone you've hurt recently.

• Talk to a parent, teacher, friend, or counselor about things that are bugging you. That way, you won't be as likely to take them out on others.

Your Imaginary Alter Ego:
Sharpay from the High School Musical movies

This drama queen is willing to **sabotage** anyone to stay in the spotlight. There is never a dull moment with Sharpay ruling from her throne!

What Would You Do?
Girls Talk Back

Get straight-up advice from girls who've been there, done that.

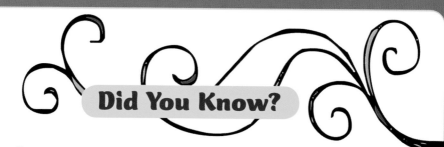

Did You Know?

★ The most current stats show that more than one out of every three students is bullied at some point during the school year. How can you do your part to bring that number down? There are lots of ways to help. You can start an anti-bullying group at school. Or you could reach out and invite someone new to have lunch with you. You could even lend an ear to someone who has been bullied. You can help just by being a good friend.

★ Be careful who you pick on—they just might become famous one day! Celebs such as Rosario Dawson, Jessica Alba, and Robert Pattinson were all bullied in their younger years.

Q: When I get jealous, I'm often mean to my BFF. I get jealous when she gets better grades or gets picked first for a team. What's a healthy way to handle it?

A: It's natural to feel jealous sometimes. Life isn't a competition, but it can feel like one at times. The way to get ahead isn't to **begrudge** your friends in the process. Next time you're green with **envy**, stop for a minute. Be honest about why you're upset. Who knows? Your friend might even be able to help you study or practice your skills in the sport of your choice. And you'll be a better friend if you support your friend in her achievements.

24 to 33 points:

THE NOT-SO-INNOCENT BYSTANDER

Could it be that you're an undercover instigator? Signs point to yes.

The Full Scoop

Your friendships mean the world to you. But maybe fitting in with the crowd means even more. At times, you'll do or say whatever it takes to be liked by the in-crowd. But sometimes your pursuit of popularity translates to bully-style behavior. Sure, it's indirect bullying, but it still has a direct impact. Also, because you're so easily influenced, you might even find yourself the target of bullying. Bystanders often recognize bullying behaviors but don't know how to stop it. You can break the mold by taking action. Next time you see a bully in action, use your voice. Bullies often listen when a bystander says, "Stop."

Real-Life Rx: Tips You Can Use

• Operation Backbone! Sometimes the need to belong keeps us from setting clear **boundaries**. Next time something doesn't feel right, trust your gut and say so. You'll earn more respect from others—and yourself.

• Express yourself and be straight up. Saying what you really mean will help keep an aggressive person at bay.

• Watching a bully in action may make you feel helpless. But speaking up can make a difference. Stats show that witnesses brave enough to tell a bully to stop succeed 50 percent of the time. You can also find a trusted adult to step in and save the day.

Your Imaginary Alter Ego:
Gretchen from *Mean Girls*

At North Shore High, the evil Plastic clique rules the school. Gretchen is the too-loyal sidekick to queen bee Regina. Gretchen goes along with just about anything Regina wants. It doesn't matter if it's ultra-mean. When Gretchen finds herself on the outside, she discovers the flip side of being a clique follower.

What Would You Do?
Girls Talk Back

Get straight-up advice from girls who've been there, done that.

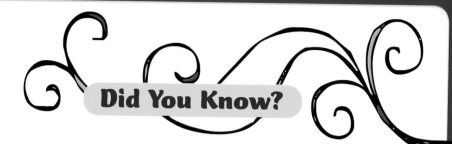

Did You Know?

⭐ Girl power is great and all, but not when it's harnessed to hurt others. More girls than guys say they are bullied at school.

⭐ Lots of bullies hide behind their computers. In fact, 42 percent of young people say they've been bullied online. If online bullying happens to you, tell your mom or dad or another trusted adult. Sometimes you can even prevent bullying from happening. Keep your passwords secret. And be careful about the photos and information you share online.

Q: My best friend suddenly stopped talking to me and won't tell me why. What do I do?

A: Being in the dark is no fun. Before your friendship turns to ice, there are a few things you can do. First, see if she's willing to meet with you alone to talk things out. Things can change on neutral ground! Also, if this is a pattern, consider letting go of this friendship for good. Some things just aren't worth worrying over. You deserve friends you can count on.

THE BULLY'S TARGET

Odds are you recognize bullying when it happens to others. But do you recognize bullying when you're the target?

The Full Scoop

You're trustworthy and reliable to a fault, which makes you an easy target for bullies. Bullies don't always hit their targets with their fists. Sometimes they use words. Those words can be hurtful comments said to you at the lunch table or in the locker room. Or they can be sent in embarrassing texts or posts to social networking sites. Everyone else may think the words are just jokes, but if they hurt you, they aren't funny. It's bullying. And you should say so. Stand up for yourself. If the bully won't listen—or you're afraid—talk to a parent or another adult who can help.

Real-Life Rx: Tips You Can Use

• You can be a really great friend. But are you being true to yourself too? If you're being bullied, stand up for yourself. You're worth it!

• Getting revenge against a bully may be tempting, but it's never a good move. It just turns you into a bully too. And it could make the bullying grow worse.

• Chances are you're not the bully's only target. Make friends with someone who is going through the same thing you're going through. And remember, two is better than one. It's easier to stand up to a bully when you have a friend by your side.

• Sometimes the situation is more than you can handle. If that's the case, don't be afraid to ask for help. Talk to a parent, teacher, or another adult. If you don't get help from the first person you try, talk to someone else.

• It's easy to start an anti-bullying program at your school. Lots of programs exist to stomp out bad bully behavior.

Your Celeb Alter Ego:
Willow Smith

Beautiful inside and out, singer Willow Smith is all about staying true to yourself. Her hit song, "Whip My Hair," talks about not allowing anyone to stop the real you from shining through! Willow is also a great role model for female friendship.

What Would You Do?
Girls Talk Back

Get straight-up advice from girls who've been there, done that.

Did You Know?

⭐ Much like you, Ellen DeGeneres is no fan of mean girls. The popular talk show host speaks out against bullies. She often airs anti-bullying video messages from famous people. (Do the names Justin Bieber and President Barack Obama ring a bell?)

⭐ Remember that bullies are people too. It's definitely not OK to bully. However, their actions might be fueled by family problems or low self-esteem. Try to have some compassion the next time you're tempted to roll your eyes at the queen bees.

Q: I just found out that a friend sent an unflattering text about me around school—complete with pictures! I'm totally embarrassed, but she's still my friend. What should I do?

A: You may be tempted to get back at your friend and send out an unflattering text about her. But don't do it! You'll only make the situation worse. And since you are a good friend, it will probably make you feel bad. The best thing to do is to talk to a parent or teacher about the situation. With their help, you could talk to your friend and let her know how her actions hurt you.

Glossary

begrudge (bee-GRUHJ)—to be jealous of someone else

boundaries (BOUN-duh-rees)—limits

clique (KLIK)—a group of friends who do not accept others into their group

envy (EN-vee)—to wish you could have something someone else has or do something that she has done

exclude (eks-KLOOD)—to keep someone from joining or taking part in something

instigator (IN-stuh-gay-tuhr)—someone who provokes another into doing something

sabotage (SAB-uh-tahzh)—to damage, destroy, or interfere with on purpose

Read More

Burstein, John. *Why are You Picking on Me?: Dealing with Bullies.* Slim Goodbody's Life Skills 101. New York: Crabtree Pub. Co., 2010.

Hewitt, Sally. *Bullying.* How Can I Deal with .... Mankato, Minn.: Black Rabbit Books, 2009.

Shapiro, Ouisie. *Bullying and Me: Schoolyard Stories.* Chicago: Albert Whitman & Company, 2010.

Internet Sites

FactHound offers a safe, fun way to find Internet sites related to this book. All of the sites on FactHound have been researched by our staff.

Here's all you do:

Visit *www.facthound.com*

Type in this code: 9781429665407

Check out projects, games and lots more at
www.capstonekids.com

31

Index